# Cliff F.L. JENKS
# &
# Phil H. LISTEMANN

**Colour artwork: Malcolm Laird**

**Layout & project design: Phil Listemann**

Copyright © Phil Listemann 2008
revised 2015

**ISBN 978-29526381-9-7**

All rights reserved. No parts of this publication may be reproduced, stored in a retrieval system or transmitted in any form or by any means, electronic, mechanical, photocopying, recording or otherwise, without permission in writing from the Authors.

ACKNOWLEDGEMENTS

Brendon Deere, Errol Martyn, Peter Mossong, Matthew O'Sullivan.

Edited by Phil H. Listemann

philedition@wanadoo.fr

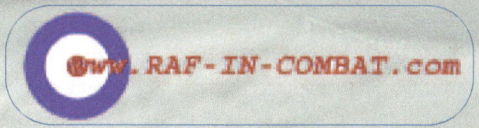

GLOSSARY OF TERMS

DFC : Distinguished Flying Cross
F/L : Flight Lieutenant
F/O : Flying Officer
F/Sgt : Flight Sergeant
MAG : Marine Air Group
P/O : Pilot Officer
PoW : Prisoner of War

RNZAF : Royal New Zealand Air Force
Sgt : Sergeant
S/L : Squadron Leader
Sqn : Squadron
USMC : United States Marince Corps
USN : United States Navy
W/O : Warrant Officer

# INTRODUCTION

A USMC SBD-5 returning from a mission over Rabaul in 1944, at the time the New Zealanders made their tour. The production batch starting with "150" was used by two USMC units in 1944, VMSB-235 and VMSB-241. By that time, the USMC was the main user of the Dauntless, while the USN was replacing the SBD with Curtiss SB2Cs. (*Brendon Deere Collection*)

The Douglas Dauntless was developed from the Northrop BT-1 as the XBT-2 and soon redesignated XSBD-1. Fitted with some improvements, the SBD-1 was introduced into service in 1940, with 54 being built for the US Marine Corps. The Dauntless was an all-metal single-engine monoplane designed to carry out either dive-bombing or scout work from aircraft carriers or land bases.

The SBD-1 was followed by the improved -2, of which 87 were delivered between December 1940 and May 1941. But it was with the next production version, the SBD-3, that the SBD became the backbone of the attack squadrons of the USN for the next two years of the Pacific war. The SBD-3 was the first fully combat-worthy Dauntless and introduced several refinements including improved armament. Introduced in March 1941, it took part in all major battles of 1942 and in all, 585 were delivered until October 1942. At that time, it was replaced on the production lines by the SBD-4, a version which introduced a new 24 volt electrical system and other refinements. The 780 -4s were built in less than six months, the last being accepted by the Navy in February 1943.

But the main production version had yet to come, the SBD-5. The first delivery took place on 21 February 1943 and was followed by 2,963 more until March 1944. Many improvements were again introduced, like a much more powerful engine, up-rated from 1,000 hp to 1,200 hp. The increased power enabled the offensive load to be increased to a maximum of 2,250 lb. Nevertheless, the Dauntless was already outdated when this version arrived at the front line, and was obsolete when the New Zealanders arrived to complete their tour of operations. It remained in front line service only because the introduction of its successor, the Curtiss SB2C was delayed for some months and because of decreasing air activity by the Japanese Navy and Army aviation from mid-1943 onwards.

However, the Dauntless remains one of the major types that fought the war in the Pacific, it achieved no such fame in other theatres. It was gradually overshadowed by other types after 1943 but soldiered on until 1945, mainly with USMC units. Its land-based version, the A-24 Banshee, saw little active service, with poor results.

Douglas SBD-3 and -4s previously of Marine Air Group 14 (MAG-14) at Seagrove in mid-1943. Most of these aircraft were later used by No.25 Squadron, RNZAF for training duties. (*Brendon Deere Collection*)

Douglas SBD-3 BuNo 4549 with the temporary RNZAF serial NZ208 painted on the rear fuselage. A few weeks later this aircraft crashed, fortunately without injury to the pilot. (*Brendon Deere Collecion*)

## TECHNICAL DATA
### DOUGLAS SBD-5

**Manufacturer:**
Douglas Aircraft Company, El Segundo California

**Type:**
Carrier-based scout/dive-bomber.

**Accommodation:**
Pilot and observer/rear gunner

**Power plant:**
One 1,200 hp air-cooled 9-cylinder Wright *Cyclone* R-1820-60

**Fuel & Oil**
*Fuel (US Gal):*
Normal capacity : 260 [984 l] &
two 65-gallon [246 l] extra tanks in each outer wing panel.

*Oil (US Gal):*
Standard : 16.50 [62.45 l]

**Dimensions:**
Span : 41 ft 6.25-in [12,66 m]
Length : 32 ft 1.25-in [9,79 m]
Height : 13 ft 7-in [4,14 m]
Wing area : 325 Sq ft [30,19 m²]

**Weights:**
*Empty* : 4,404 lb [2 905 kg]
*Loaded* : 9,359 lb [4 245 kg]
*MTOW* : 10,700 [4 853 kg]

**Performance:**
*Max speed :*
255 mph at 14,000 ft
[410 km/h at 4 265 m]

*Cruising speed* : 185 mph [298 km/h]

*Service ceiling* : 25,530 ft [7 780 m]

*Normal range* : 1,115 miles [1 795 km]

*Endurance at cruising speed :*
6h00

**Armament:**
2 x fixed forward-firing 0.50-in [12.7mm] with 200 rpg.
2 x flexible dorsal 0.30-in [7.62 mm] with 500 rpg.

*provision for :*
1,600 lb [726 kg] bomb under the fuselage
and
two 325 lb [147.5 kg] bombs under the wings

## Dauntless Dive Bombers for New Zealand

As a loyal member of the British Commonwealth, New Zealand had dispatched a considerable number of army and air force personnel to bolster Britain's perilous position in the Middle East and elsewhere during 1940-41. However, after Japan's December 1941 attack on Pearl Harbour and rapid advance to within striking distance of Australia, New Zealand suddenly found itself dangerously close to the front line.

Despite having a population of only two million during the Second World War, New Zealand was ready to play her part, but was woefully short of modern aircraft. Improvements began when the RNZAF was integrated into the American South Pacific Command (SOPAC) and deliveries of modern US warplanes commenced - some diverted from British orders.

Within a year, the number of RNZAF squadrons had increased sevenfold and by the end of 1944, 80% of the RNZAF home based squadrons had been transferred to offensive operations in the SW Pacific theatre. Twenty eight squadrons saw active service in the Pacific before the war ended.

Unlike other allied air forces, the RNZAF received most for its Lend-Lease equipment directly from US Navy inventory. Indeed, requisitions depended on the concurrence of the local Allied Forces Commander, and for the RNZAF, this meant US Navy Rear Admiral Ghormley.

As the RNZAF Squadrons were to fight alongside US Marine Corps units flying SBDs, an order for 120 A-24Bs (42-54766/54885), the Army version of the Dauntless, was cancelled in January 1944 and replaced by SBDs. Hence, the US Navy, US Marines, the RNZAF and the French AF in 1944-45, were the only Allied air forces to fly the Dauntless in combat.

The idea of equipping the RNZAF with Dauntless dive-bombers was first mooted in February, 1943. At that time, the Allied forces under the command of General MacArthur, were firmly established on the island of Bougainville and in the western half of New Britain - positions which allowed the heavily defended Japanese base at Rabaul to be attacked from both east and west. However, despite a prolonged and intensive bombing campaign throughout 1943, Rabaul - although weakened - remained a formidable fortress.

Since a direct assault would require massive sea and land forces and could result in heavy casualties, the decision was taken in early 1944, to step up the air campaign even further before committing ground troops. The RNZAF offered to provide additional squadrons and, under the original plan, Nos. 25, 26, 27 and 28 were to be equipped with the Dauntless. In the event, only No.25 Squadron used the type operationally as more modern types became available.

The RNZAF used three variants of the Dauntless, the SBD-3 and 4 for training, all on loan from the US Marines, and the SBD-5, which was used on operations by No. 25 Squadron.

### THE SBDs OF THE RNZAF

| NZ Serial | Previous | BuNo | On loan | Wfu |
|---|---|---|---|---|
| **SBD-3** | | | | |
| NZ5001 | NZ205 | 06651 | 03.11.43 | Feb-44 |
| NZ5002 | NZ206 | 06652 | 26.10.43 | Feb-44 |
| NZ5003 | NZ207 | 4672 | 21.10.43 | Feb-44 |
| NZ5004 | NZ208 | 4559 | 03.11.43 | 19.01.44 |
| NZ5005 | NZ209 | 4585 | 03.11.43 | Feb-44 |
| NZ5006 | NZ210 | 03371 | 26.10.43 | Feb-44 |
| NZ5007 | NZ211 | 03219 | ? | 13.09.43 |
| NZ5008 | NZ212 | 4675 | ? | Feb-44 |
| NZ5009 | NZ213 | 4652 | 03.11.43 | Feb-44 |
| NZ5010 | NZ214 | 06658 | 03.11.43 | Feb-44 |
| NZ5011 | NZ215 | 03202 | 14.11.43 | Feb-44 |
| NZ5012 | NZ216 | 4645 | 03.11.43 | Feb-44 |
| NZ5013 | NZ217 | 03364 | 03.11.43 | Feb-44 |
| NZ5014 | NZ218 | 03364 | 03.11.43 | Feb-44 |
| NZ5015 | NZ219 | 06649 | 03.11.43 | Feb-44 |
| NZ5016 | NZ220 | 06545 | 13.11.43 | Feb-44 |
| NZ5017 | NZ221 | 03369 | 03.11.43 | Feb-44 |
| NZ5018 | NZ222 | 06519 | ? | Feb-44 |
| **SBD-4** | | | | |
| NZ5019 | - | 10389 | 14.11.43 | Feb-44 |
| NZ5020 | - | 10632 | 14.11.43 | Feb-44 |
| NZ5021 | - | 10508 | 14.11.43 | Feb-44 |
| NZ5022 | - | 10345 | 14.11.43 | Feb-44 |
| NZ5023 | - | 10582 | 14.11.43 | Feb-44 |
| NZ5024 | - | 10539 | 14.11.43 | Feb-44 |
| NZ5025 | - | 10691 | 14.11.43 | Feb-44 |
| NZ5026 | - | 10599 | 13.11.43 | Feb-44 |
| NZ5027 | - | 10583 | 13.11.43 | Feb-44 |
| NZ5028 | - | 06952 | 17.12.43 | Feb-44 |
| NZ5029 | - | 10535 | 17.12.43 | Feb-44 |
| NZ5030 | - | 06744 | 17.12.43 | Feb-44 |
| NZ5031 | - | 10407 | 17.12.43 | Feb-44 |
| NZ5032 | - | 10404 | 17.12.43 | Feb-44 |
| NZ5033 | - | 06740 | 17.12.43 | Feb-44 |
| NZ5034 | - | 06766 | 17.12.43 | Feb-44 |
| NZ5035 | - | 06763 | 17.12.43 | Feb-44 |
| NZ5036 | - | 06815 | 17.12.43 | Feb-44 |
| NZ5037 | - | 06953 | 26.12.43 | 12.02.44 |
| NZ5038 | - | 10393 | 26.12.43 | Feb-44 |
| NZ5039 | - | 06931 | 26.12.43 | Feb-44 |
| NZ5040 | - | 10607 | 26.12.43 | Feb-44 |
| NZ5041 | - | 06961 | 30.12.43 | Feb-44 |
| NZ5042 | - | 10384 | 08.01.44 | Feb-44 |
| NZ5043 | - | 10636 | 08.01.44 | Feb-44 |
| NZ5044 | - | 06789 | 26.01.44 | Feb-44 |
| NZ5045 | - | 10500 | 26.01.44 | Feb-44 |

For No. 25 Squadron crews, training on the type began with war-weary SBD-3s like this one, NZ5006, which was repainted with RNZAF roundels.
*(Brendon Deere Collection)*

## No. 25 Squadron, RNZAF
### July 1943 - May 1944

No. 25 Squadron was formed specifically to fly one type of aircraft, the Douglas SBD Dauntless. Operating alongside US Air Force and Marine Corps Units, No.25 completed one operational tour against one major target - the Japanese base at Rabaul on the island of New Britain.

Created on 31 July 1943, at Seagrove near Auckland, on New Zealand's North Island, No. 25 Squadron, RNZAF, was allotted twelve aircrews and a handful of ground staff under the command of Squadron Leader T.J. McLean de Lange.

It was initially equipped with nine war weary ex US Marine Corps SBD-3 and -4 aircraft. The nine Douglas SBD-3s were on loan from MAG-14 (Marine Air Group) of the USMC who were then based at Seagrove for a period of rest and recuperation. The SBD-3s - referred to by the American pilots as 'Slow But Deadly' due to its ability to absorb battle damage - were combat-weary and it took a full week's work before the Squadron could get it's first SBD airborne. In addition, spares were in short supply and several machines had to be cannibalised with the help of mechanics from MAG-14 to restore the remainder to flying condition. The maintenance problems continued to hamper training, with a 40% serviceability rate being the norm!

The Squadron's requests for better aircraft were finally answered at the end of September when the number of SBDs was increased to 17. Eighteen aircraft were delivered (RNZAF serials NZ205 - NZ222) plus a further batch in November 1943 (NZ5019 - NZ5027).

NZ211 crashed during a training flight on 13 September 1943 near Waiuku, North Island, NZ, killing both the pilot, Flying Officer W.D. McJannett and gunner, Sergeant D.M.J. Cairns. Despite being struck off charge, NZ211 was subsequently renumbered as NZ5007.

By August, these aircraft began to receive temporary RNZAF serial numbers (NZ205-NZ222) but by late November or early December, had been allocated full RNZAF serials (NZ5001-NZ5018). A further nine aircraft were borrowed and received RNZAF serials, NZ5019-NZ5027.

At this time, many were repainted in similar colours, but with the addition of Blue/White/Blue RNZAF roundels without White bars, in six positions. Those on the fuselage sides had a Yellow outer ring as per contemporary RAF fuselage roundels. Fin flashes do not appear to have been added to the aircraft at this time, but the last number of the serial was added in White to the fin and the nose cowl of most aircraft.

### CONVERSION TRAINING

For the rest of the year the training continued and, bit by bit, a full complement of aircrew were transferred into the Squadron. None of the New Zealand pilots had any experience of flying dive-bombers. The first batch of pilots had come from Army Co-operation squadrons or from second-line units and later they were joined by pilots fresh from flying school. As for the air gunners, most had arrived from Canada where they had been

Some New Zealanders pilots and air gunners posing in front an ex USMC Dauntless at Seagrove. From left to right, are believed to be : Flight Sergeants N.L. Kelly and B.E. Cullen, Flying Officer G.C. Howie, Flight Sergeants J.S.R. Roberston, O.E. Watson, L.H. Jolly, N.G. Silver, Pilot Officer G.H. Grey, Flying Officer F.G. McKenzie and Pilot Officer G.H. French. Graham Howie was later killed late in the war in a Corsair crash (NZ5394) on 13 June 1945 whislt serving with No.16 Squadron, RNZAF in the South Pacific. (*Air Force Museum PR1570*)

sent under the Empire Training Scheme; others were assigned from bomber and coastal patrol squadrons for a new operational tour.

After an intensive ground course, flight training commenced. To convert to the Dauntless pilots had to complete a minimum of 60 hours. The programme included dive-bombing practice, a hair-raising experience for the crews, especially the rear-gunner who had to sit with his back to the engine in a dive at 75 degrees from the horizontal. Alternative modes of attack were the 'semi-vertical' dive at 45 degrees without the perforated trailing-edge air-brakes extended, and the low-level bombing run between 500/1500ft (150/500m).

In addition there was live firing practice for both pilot and air gunner, formation flying and day/night navigation exercises. To mark the completion of their training, a formation of 18 aircraft flew over Auckland on the morning of 16 January 1944. At this time, this was the largest formation of aircraft ever seen over the city.

All Squadron personnel were then dispatched to Swanson for infantry weapons training and a course in jungle warfare/survival. There was more to come - operational training under tropical conditions at Pallikulo airbase on the island of Esperitu Santo in the New Hebrides (now Vanuatu). The ground echelon (No. 25 Servicing Unit) had been sent ahead to prepare for their reception. On 30 January, 1944, the aircrews of No. 25 Squadron left New Zealand aboard a Lockheed Lodestar and Douglas Dakota of No.40 Squadron, RNZAF, arriving at Pallikulo nine hours later where they found a line-up of 27 newer, but still well worn, ex USMC SBD-4s (RNZAF serials NZ5019 - NZ5045) to replace the worn out -3s they had left in New Zealand.

## MORE OPERATIONAL TRAINING

The next day, operational training resumed - more dive-bombing practice and live gunnery exercises, formation and instrument flying. On 11 February 1944, during an instrument flying session, the squadron lost it's first aircraft when SBD-4 NZ5037, flown by Flying Officer A. Moore and Flight Sergeant J.K. Munro, went missing. Despite widespread searches over the following days, neither the aircraft or crew were found. More than forty years later, in 1987, the wreck of the missing SBD was discovered 50km from Santo. There was no trace of the crew. The aircraft was subsequently salvaged and restored as a museum exhibit.

Training continued throughout February, culminating in mock sorties with US Marine Corps units (MAG-11, MAG-12 and MAG-21) where the New Zealanders were only a small part of formations that, at times, numbered over 100 aircraft.

Various scenes of the training of the New Zealander crews in New Zealand. Above a crew in NZ5003 and below NZ5005, two SBD-3s which were used by the RNZAF for a couple of months only.

Two more SBDs which were used for training in New Zealand, NZ2014, a SBD-3 and below NZ2025, a SBD-4.

Three SDB-3s (NZ5001, NZ5013 and NZ5014) flying in formation over the New Zealand countryside. By late 1943, the Dauntless was clearly obsolete, that is why only one RNZAF squadron eventually operated the type. Better weapons were already available to the Allies by then, like the Corsair, a versatile aircraft the New Zealanders were soon to receive. (*Brendon Deere Collection*)

Towards the end of the month, No. 25 Squadron began to receive brand new Douglas SBD-5s to replace their second-hand SBD-4s. These were from the Marine Corps stocks (NZ5046-NZ5063) and were operated from 19 February 1944 in Marine Corps markings. By 25 February they had been repainted with RNZAF roundels in four positions, and RNZAF serial numbers. All appeared to have the large pneumatic tailwheel fitted to land based USMC aircraft. The old machines were handed back to the Americans at the beginning of March.

From that moment on, training was over and No. 25 Squadron was considered combat-ready. Their first mission had been scheduled for the end of February but this was postponed until 22 March 1944, because the Squadron's forward base at Piva on Bougainville was under repeated bombardment from Japanese artillery. Apart from a few familiarisation flights, there was very little activity at Pallikulo while the squadron waited for the ground situation to be resolved.

### Target: Guadalcanal!

On the morning of 22 March, the order came through to pack up and head for Piva via Henderson Field on Guadalcanal - a long detour south across open sea. No. 25 Squadron flew the first leg in two echelons of nine aircraft - each led by a Lockheed PV-1 from No. 9 Squadron, RNZAF.

After a flight lasting five hours, all the New Zealand pilots reached Henderson Field but, on landing, Flying Officer B.N. Graham swerved off the runway and collided with a petrol bowser, writing off his SBD-5 NZ5055. The following day, the first nine aircraft, led by Squadron Leader McLean de Lange, reached Piva without incident and the second nine arriving on 24 March.

Soon after landing, Squadron Leader McLean de Lange set about organising an operational sortie. This was a fairly timid artillery spotting exercise. The first aircraft (NZ5049) piloted by Flying Officer L.A. McLellan-Symonds took off at 0545, followed one hour later by the squadron commander himself and his rear gunner, Flying Officer Sewell. The CO was the first to come back at 0825, Flying Officer McLellan-Symonds landing 40 minutes late without incident. At 0950 six aircraft were provided as part of a force of 18 SBDs and 9 TBFs for a strike on beach and inland targets at Tavera. Only four NZ aircraft, led by Flying Officer F.G. McKenzie and his gunner (NZ5061) took off on the mission but all dropped their bombs in the target area.

In the early afternoon, five aircraft were included in a force of 18 SBDs and three TBFs for a strike just outside the airfield perimeter. This attack, led by the B flight commander, Flight Lieutenant T.R.F. Johnson, was unique for two reasons. First, it was possible for the ground crew, who had just refuelled and rearmed the aircraft, to see bombs falling from the same aircraft as they attacked the Japanese positions. Secondly, the leading American SBD carried an officer of the Fiji 1st Battalion as observer. This officer, Lieutenant Viggers, advised the formation leader on which positions to attack. Later, at 1710,

Line-up of SBD-4s (first two) and SBD-3s (the next two) at Seagrove. The first machine has no "last two" digits painted in yellow on the cowling, whilst most of the others do. It seems that not all SBDs received such marking which normally also appeared on the tail. In February and March 1944 alone, almost 700 hours of flying was performed by the squadron, mostly on these war-weary machines. *(Brendon Deere Collection)*

Flight Lieutenant Johnson was airborne again leading six aircraft this time, again with Lieutenant Viggers as observer, attacked the same target. As a result of this attack the Squadron suffered its first aircraft damage. Flight Sergeants Kelly and B. Cullen brought back NZ5062 with one bullet hole in the rudder. Including the two artillery spotting flights performed mid-day, the Squadron performed 19 sorties that day, a good start for the Kiwis.

The following day, two strikes were carried out on local gun positions, both took place before mid-day. In each case the strike force was 9 SBDs and 6 TBFs and the Squadron provided all the SBDs. In the second strike at least, the TBF's were from No.30 Squadron, RNZAF. Results were quite successful and at least one gun emplacement was completely destroyed. The day ended with two artillery spotting flights which were carried out led by A Flight leader, Flight Lieutenant J.W. Edwards, but Flight Sergeant Kelly and his gunner (NZ5062) had to return owing to fuel trouble. The target was an ammunition dump and supply area at Talili Bay. The strike was very successful and a large amount of damage was caused.

Later in the afternoon a force of 12 SBDs and 9 TBFs attacked Japanese positions three miles inland from the mouth of the Maririci river. Because of dense foliage results were difficult to assess. Half of the SBDs were from the Squadron, which were led this time by the other flight leader, Flight Lieutenant T.R.F. Johnson. Lakunai airfield runway and gun positions were the targets for a Rabaul strike force of 36 SBDs, 24 TBFs and 8 escorts for the 28 March 1944. The Squadron provided 11 aircraft led the CO but two of these aborted (Sergeant C.G.W. Khun / Flight Sergeant M. Small - NZ5053 and Sergeant P.R.B. Symonds /

Squadron Leader T.J. McLean de Lange, CO of No. 25 Squadron, seated in NZ5057, with his air gunner, Flying Officer L.T. Sewell. Born in India, McLean de Lange was educated in England before moving to New Zealand. He served as a regular officer with the RNZAF from 1938 to 1966, retiring with the rank of Air Commodore. For his outstanding command of the only dive-bombing squadron of the RNZAF, he was awarded the DFC on 29 September 1944.
(Air Force Museum PR3447)

by mixed crews of Kiwi pilot (Sergeants Khun and Forsberg) and USMC observer on board two USMC SBDs (#181 and 177). March 26th should have been Squadron's first long range strike, but it became an abortive one. The target was Kavieng airfield, New Ireland and the force from Piva was 36 SBDs, 12 TBFs and 8 escorts. In addition 18 SBDs and 12 TBFs based at Green Island were to co-ordinate in the attack. The Squadron provided 12 aircraft but after leaving Green Island these, plus 6 American SBDs failed to rendezvous with the rest of the strike force due to poor weather conditions and returned to Green Island after 2.5 hours flying. After a brief landing they flew back to Piva. The next day, at 0850 a strike force of 28 SBDs, 22 TBFs and 8 escorts were airborne for a strike on Rabaul. The Squadron contribution was six aircraft, Flight Sergeant B. Boden - NZ5049) because of engine trouble and instrument trouble. AA fire was moderate to intense but not very accurate. NZ5046 (Flying Officer L.H.F. Brown / Flight Sergeant G.D. Ashworth) came home with several machine gun bullet holes in the tail-plane. The next day was a quiet day for the Kiwis and only six aircraft, led by Flight Lieutenant Johnson (of a force of 27 SBDs, 18 TBFs and 8 escorts) were airborne for a strike on the Vanapope area. The NZ aircraft attacked automatic AA positions, scoring three damaging hits.

On 30 March, gun positions around Vunakanau airfield received attention from 36 SBDs, 24 TBFs and 8 escorts. All in all it was not a very successful mission. The SBDs were hampered by cloud which partially obscured the target and only 10 hits were recorded. Also, bombs carried by two RNZAF aircraft failed to

## THE SBDs OF THE RNZAF

### SBD-5

| NZ Serial | BuNo | Returned |
|---|---|---|
| NZ5046 | 36862 | 20.05.44 |
| NZ5047 | 36891 | 20.05.44 |
| NZ5048 | 36895 | 20.05.44 |
| NZ5049 | 36897 | 20.05.44 |
| NZ5050 | 36898 | - |
| NZ5051 | 36908 | - |
| NZ5052 | 36910 | 20.05.44 |
| NZ5053 | 36911 | 20.05.44 |
| NZ5054 | 36914 | - |
| NZ5055 | 36923 | - |
| NZ5056 | 36924 | 20.05.44 |
| NZ5057 | 36925 | 20.05.44 |
| NZ5058 | 36928 | - |
| NZ5059 | 36916 | - |
| NZ5060 | 28516 | 20.05.44 |
| NZ5061 | 28526 | 20.05.44 |
| NZ5062 | 28536 | 20.05.44 |
| NZ5063 | 10849 | 20.05.44 |
| NZ5064 | 54201 | 20.05.44 |
| NZ5065 | 54212 | 20.05.44 |
| NZ5066 | 28435 | 20.05.44 |
| NZ5067 | 10895 | 20.05.44 |
| NZ5068 | 35923 | 20.05.44 |

release. Although AA fire was almost non-existent, small arms fire was responsible for a shattered canopy on NZ5050 (Pilot Officer G.H. Cray / Flight Sergeant F.D. Bell). A US SBD was successfully ditched on the way to the target and the crew rescued by a Catalina. This was the first mission in which No.25 Squadron led the SBD force, and 12 aircraft were provided under the command of Squadron Leader McLean de Lange.

On the last day of the month, the Squadron's 12 aircraft, under the command of Flight Lieutenant J.W. Edwards, joined with three other squadrons to give a total of 54 SBDs for a strike on the gun positions around Lakunai airfield. The force, including 18 TBFs and 8 escorts, took off at 1000 for an attack timed for 1200. The results were fairly successful and the New Zealanders scored five of the fifteen hits recorded.

### First Combat Losses

So far, the first missions were carried without any major incident, but things changed with April. On the first day of that month, the Kiwis were on duty again. The supply and bivouac area on the Maririoi river was again the target for a Squadron strike. In mid-morning, with Squadron Leader McLean de Lange being the formation leader, and again in mid-afternoon led by Flight Lieutenant Edwards, a force of 6 Kiwi SBDs and 6 TBFs struck the area. As with previous strikes, the results were hard to assess, and the afternoon strike was hampered by showery weather.

The following day, 54 SBDs, 24 TBFs and 8 escorts combined with 12 aircraft from Green Island to attack gun positions at Rabaul. Cloud over the target forced the mission to attack the secondary target which was Raluana Point, buildings, gun positions and the barge area in Keravia Bay were all struck with moderate success. AA was light and inaccurate. This strike was the first on which the SBDs carried 2 x 125 lb fragmentation clusters. NZ5054 (Flight Sergeants L.H. Jolly and T.E. Price) and NZ5059 (Sergeant P.R.B. Symonds and Flight Sergeant B. Boden), both had hang-ups of these clusters which exploded during the landing at Piva. Flight Sergeant Jolly was unhurt but the other three crew members were all injured. Both aircraft were burnt beyond repair and this was the last time that SBDs carried that type of armament.

On 3 April, Squadron Leader McLean de Lange led 60 SBDs, including 12 aircraft from the Squadron in a strike on Vunakanau. Also taking part were 24 TBFs and 8 escorts. Cloud cover of 70% made accurate bombing difficult and although some hits were recorded results were generally not assessable. Some of the aircraft attacked the Tobera airfield in lieu of their assigned target. One Squadron aircraft (NZ5053) did not take part in the strike because of engine trouble.

The 4 April, 1944 was a very sad day for No. 25 Squadron, as the Squadron lost its first aircrew. In the morning Flying Officer L.A. McLellan-Symonds in a US aircraft "161" and Flying Officers B.N. Graham and G.C. Howie in NZ5048, flew via Munda (near Ondonga) to Henderson Field, Guadalcanal, in order to pick up two aircraft. The aircraft were in US markings and codes, Flying Officer L.A. McLellan-Symonds piloting "176", Flying Officer B.N. Graham in "14" and Flying Officer G.C. Howie in NZ5048. They took off at 1410 and shortly afterwards landed at Russell Island to refuel before flying direct to Piva. On the way to Piva they experienced radio transmission difficulties between themselves and on ETA they could see no land. The weather started to deteriorate and darkness was not far off when the wingmen recognised the coast of New Britain. Because of the radio problem they could not let Flying Officer McLellan-Symonds know where they were and he thought he was still lost. They turned back and were headed for Green Island when, inexplicably, Flying Officer McLellan-Symonds broke formation. Although Air Sea Rescue received a transmission of an intended ditching, he was never seen again. After the war, it was discovered that McLellan-Symonds had been captured by the Japanese and held in the POW camp at Tunnel Hill Road where he died from blood-poisoning on 25 May 1944. The other two aircraft landed safely at Green Island, about an hour after dark.

After one day without operations due to poor weather, the Squadron was back to work on 6 April. Vunakanau was again the target for a force of 66 SBDs (12 from the Squadron led by Flight Lieutenant Edwards), 24 TBFs and 8 escorts and again cloud intervened, so the force attacked the secondary target, the Talili Bay supply area. Results were fair and many direct hits were reported on buildings, gun positions and one on an oil storage tank. Moderate AA fire caused no damage to the SBDs. The next day the New Zealanders provided only 6 aircraft for a strike on Rabaul by 42 SBDs, 36 TBFs and 8 escorts. The target was gun positions in the Talili Bay area and the result was three guns destroyed and six damaged.

On 8 April, 48 SBDs, 17 TBFs and 8 escorts struck gun positions along the ridge near Rataval. Out of 14 hits reported by the SBDs the six NZ aircraft accounted for five. AA fire was fairly intense and accurate but apart from a few small holes the SBDs got off lightly. While this was going on five other NZ SBDs were in a force of 12 which struck at gun positions 1,000 yards west of the Mamagata river. Two aircraft scored direct hits on a pill

As Flight Commander, Flight Lieutenant T.R.F. Johnson (left) played a major role, often leading the Kiwis in combat. Flight Sergeant R.J. Howell, his air gunner is on the right. Like Graham Howie, Thomas Johnson started another tour with No.16 Squadron, RNZAF in South Pacific, and was killed on 15 January 1945, flying Corsair NZ5283. He was one of eight Kiwi Corsair pilots lost that day, one of the blackest day for the RNZAF fighting in the Pacific.

box and one of these was the CO's aircraft, NZ5057.

The following day, the Japanese received a visit from 60 SBDs, 24 TBFs and 6 escorts led by Squadron Leader McLean de Lange and eleven other Squadron aircraft for a very successful attack on Vunakanau gun positions. Known positions gave little AA opposition but four new positions were found which were putting up an intensive barrage, damaging 8 SBDs. NZ5051 (Flight Lieutenant J.W. Edwards / Flight Sergeant L.A. Hoppe) had its starboard wing and tailplane extensively damaged and the radio aerial shot away, while NZ5048 (Flying Officer G.C. Howie / Flight Sergeant J.S.R. Robertson) sported a hole in the rear fuselage. On the way to the target a Zeke or possibly a Hamp was seen off Cape St George.

## More and More Missions

On 10 April, an approach at 12,500 ft from the South West was made on Raluana Point and Vunapope. The SBDs dived 9,000 ft, released bombs at 2,500 ft and leveled off at 1,500 ft, strafing islands in St. George's Channel on the way out. Moderate AA fire greeted the aircraft and NZ5047 (Flying Officer L.H.F. Brown / Flight Sergeant Ashworth), NZ5049 (Flight Lieutenant T.R.F. Johnson / Flight Sergeant R.J. Howell) and NZ5061 (Flying Officer F.G. McKenzie / Pilot Officer G.H. French) all received holes in various control surfaces.

The Squadron provided 12 aircraft, one of which aborted the mission early (NZ5053 - Sergeant C.G.W. Khun / Flight Sergeant M. Small), but most of the rest struck at the Vunapope target. 18 TBFs co-ordinated in the attack and both targets were fairly well covered with bombs. A possible Hamp was again seen off Cape St George and on the run into the target two NZ gunners, Flight Sergeant D.W. Gray (NZ5056) am Flight Sergeant T.E. Price (NZ5060) sighted four *Zekes* over Vunakanau. The rising sun markings were clearly visible as the Zekes sat just above and 1,000 yards to the port of the SBD formation. After about half a minute they broke away with no attempt to intercept the allied force.

On April 11th, 12th and 13th, the Kiwis supplied each time 12 aircraft and several hits were confirmed. The next day, two Squadron aircraft were detailed as spares for a strike on Vunakanau. In the event their services were called upon. Among the crewmen, were the new comers Flight Lieutenant J.R. Penniket and Flying Officer J.H. Brady who had arrived from Guadalcanal on the 12th to gain combat experience. Peniket was a possible C.O. of the proposed new dive-bombing squadron, No. 26. Although even then, the formation of this unit, had already been postponed. A small force of 3 Kiwi SBDs and 3 TBFs attacked coastal guns at Buka Passage. The guns were not deterred by the bombing but ceased firing after strafing runs were made. NZ5065 (Flight Sergeants W.O. Nicholson and R.W. Cullen) was holed by shrapnel in the port wing and starboard tank.

The targets for 15 April, were Gun positions surrounding Lakunai which received a pounding from 48 SBDs and the runway was well covered by 36 TBFs. Squadron Leader T.J. McLean de Lange led the SBDs with the usual NZ contribution of 12 while 8 escort fighters accompanied the bombers. NZ5064 (Flying Officer B.N. Graham / Sergeant O.E. Watson) and NZ5053 (Sergeant C.G.W. Kuhn and Flight Sergeant M. Small) were both damaged by explosive shells. The following day, 52 SBDs carried a different bomb load of one 500 lb and two 250 lb bombs. Targets were gun positions and the runway at Vunakanau. Many hits were scored including 96 on the runway. 18 TBFs attacked the same targets and the Squadron provided 12 SBDs. One 250 lb bomb fell off NZ5057, the CO's aircraft, during take off... fortunately it did not explode but provided a heart-stopping moment.

Bomb loads were mixed on 17 April, and two of the 12 Kiwi SBDs reverted to carrying one 1,000 lb bomb. 48 SBDs, 30 TBFs and 8 escorts comprised the force which struck gun positions and the runway at Lakunai. The strike was a success but AA was fairly intense and NZ5050, which was last seen at high speed over the target area, did not rendezvous afterwards. It was believed to have been shot down with its crew, Pilot Officer G.H.Cray and Flight Sergeant F.D.Bell being reported missing. Another SBD, NZ5058 (Sergeant A.C.L. Forsberg / Flight Sergeant E.G. Leatham) received extensive damage in this raid - so much that it was considered beyond economical repair and was written off.

The Squadron was airborne the next two days providing 6 and 9 aircraft, but bad weather prevented any take-off on the 20th and 21st. On 22 April 1944, weather again took a hand and prevented a force of 54 SBDs, 24 TBFs and 8 escorts from attacking either their primary (Vunakanau) or secondary (Lakunai) targets. As a result Rapopo airfield was extensively damaged and of the 12 NZ aircraft leading the strike (led by Squadron's CO), 11 reported direct hits on the runway and the other one on a building. AA fire was very meager. Missions on the two following days were also cancelled due to bad weather, and it was only the 25th that another mission could be carried out. That day, escorted by 8 fighters, 48 SBDs and 18 TBFs bombed gun positions in the vicinity of Lakunai airfield. No.25 Squadron provided 12 aircraft (led by Flight Lieutenant J.W. Edwards) and one of the SBDs, NZ5061 (Flight Lieutenant J.R. Penniket / Flying Officer L.H.F. Brown), brought back a souvenir of the raids in the form of a piece of shrapnel in the flaps near the starboard wing root.

The following day, The runway at Vunakanau received 62 direct hits from 46 SBDs and 24 TBFs plus 8 escorting fighters. Ten kiwi aircraft led the formation (commanded by Squadron Leader McLean de Lange). Two others did not take off because of engine trouble, NZ5060 and NZ5066. NZ5049 (Flight Lieutenant T.R.F. Johnson /Flight Sergeant R.J. Howell) had it's propeller badly damaged by a shell burst and had to land at Green Island. After yet another day grounded by bad weather, the Squadron tried to strike Lakunia airfield on the 28th but the formation turned back because of the weather, once again. At last, weather was on the Allied side on 29 April when 36 SBDs (12 from the Squadron) 24 TBFs and 4 escorting fighters switched their attention to targets on Buka Island. The formation bombed two targets, military barracks at Tahitahi Point and native huts at Lonahan Village. Several direct hits were scored. April ended with 12 sorties flown to provide artillery reconnaissance in the perimeter area.

The SBDs of the Marines Corps taxiing prior another strike against the Japanese. For this kind of raid, the Kiwis often teamed up in larger formations alongside USMC Dauntlesses and USN Avengers. (*Brendon Deere Collection*)

## Towards the End of the Tour

The first day of May began with local artillery reconnaissance. The next day, in a glide bombing attack on the runway at Tobera, SBDs alone dropped 100 bombs on the runway. The 12 NZ aircraft led the strike and all but one hit the runway with their load of one 1,000 lb and two 100 lb bombs. On 3 May, Vunakanau was relatively clear of cloud and the force bombed the runway, surrounding buildings, gun positions and even the bridge at the mouth of the Warangoi river. AA damaged several aircraft including NZ5060 (Flight Sergeants L.H. Jolly and R.F. Bailey), NZ5063 (Flight Lieutenant J.R. Penniket / Flying Officer J.H. Brady) and NZ5066 (Flight Sergeants J.C. Evison and H.A. Sharp). The force consisted of 36 SBDs, 24 TBFs and 4 escorts, and was led by No. 25 Squadron aircraft. After an abortive attempt on the 4th, with a mission cancelled because of the weather, six SBDs of the Squadron (led by McLean de Lange) were assigned to a heavy AA position near Mt Boeder and the Muguai Mission on the 5th. Because of cloud Mt Boeder could not be located and all aircraft dropped through a gap in the cloud in the Mission area with unobserved results. In the afternoon a further 6 aircraft (led by Flight Lieutenant T.R.F. Johnson) sought out coastal guns and a searchlight near Sorum, on the north-east coast of Bougainville. They had a little more success than the morning mission and dropped their bombs on a clearing about 3 miles south of Sorum. Results were unobserved.

The following day, despite a 50-mile weather diversion en route it was CAVU over the supply area at Rataval and 24 SBDs and 18 TBFs plus 4 escorts attacked but with only limited success. One exception was Flight Sergeant O'Neill and his gunner Flight Sergeant Gray in NZ5056. Flying with in the

Pilot Officer L.A. McLellan-Symonds (right) was the only member of the dive-bombing squadron to become a prisoner of war, he died six weeks after capture of toxaemia. It must be recalled that the living conditions in Japanese camps were terrible and many Allied prisoners died of illness or poor treatments. Left, his gunner, R.F. Bailey.

SBD-5 NZ5056 "Paddy's mistake", all bombed-up, ready for another mission. Its crew was Flight Sergeants C.N. O'Neill and D.W. Gray. *(Brendon Deere Collection)*

leading 12 New Zealander aircraft he scored a direct hit on a petrol dump. An immense explosion occurred and a sheet of flame was seen followed by black smoke billowing to 4,000 ft. The flames died down after 5 minutes but the smoke was visible from 25 miles away.

On 7 May, military installations on Bantan Island, South Bougainville, were dive-bombed by six Squadron aircraft while two US SBDs with photographers aboard accompanied them. Extensive cloud hampered the operation. Before the end of the day, the Squadron carried out 12 local artillery reconnaissance sorties. The next day was not a big day for the New Zealanders, as six aircraft were ordered on a mission to bomb and strafe coastal guns at Cape Friendship, South Bougainville. One of these had to turn back (NZ5052 - Flight Sergeants L.H. Jolly and R.F. Bailey) with engine trouble and the other five had no success in finding the guns although AA fire was observed. The target area was bombed with no apparent result. TBFs also struck the area about the same time.

### Last Loss

The next mission came two days later, on 10 May. Back to Lakunai and gun positions close by, and on "Hospital Ridge". This time, the barrage of flak is even more intense than before. NZ5051, flown by Flight Lieutenant J.W. Edwards and his gunner Flight Sergeant L.A. Hoppe - were reportedly hit by flak just after releasing their bomb and crashed into the sea off Great Harbour, killing both crewmen. It was a cruel blow, just a week before the Squadron was due to pack its bags. The strike was led by 12 Kiwi aircraft (Squadron Leader McLean de Lange), the total force being 18 SBDs, 12 TBFs and 4 escorts. The weather over Vunakanau was unsuitable for the mission of 11 May, so the force of 48 SBDs and 24 TBFs with 4 escorts, attacked secondary targets at Tobera, and Marawaka (south of Piva). The leading 6 American SBDs were armed with eight 5" rockets but in the circumstances did not use them. New Zealand SBDs attacked as follows: Eight hit the Marawak area, three dropped their bombs on the bridge over the Warangoi river (New Britain) and one, experiencing engine trouble, jettisoned its bomb and landed at Green Island.

The next day targets, all around Rabaul area, were assigned to a combined force of 48 SBDs and 24 TBFs. Escorting aircraft numbered 12. AA was fairly light and strikes were made in most areas from Talili Bay to beyond Raluana Point. No.25 Squadron provided 12 aircraft and NZ5067 suffered slight damage (Flight Sergeants A.C.L. Forsberg and E.G. Leatham). All SBDs and TBFs landed at Green Island after the attack to refuel and

Pilot Officer G.H. Cray and Flight Sergeant F.D. Bell were the first No. 25 Squadron members killed in action, believed to have been shot down by Anti-Aircraft Artillery. (*Air Force Museum PR3467*)

bomb up for another strike on the way home. The targets were native villages on the coast south of Sorum where practically all the bombs fell in the target area.

After two artillery reconnaissance sorties on the 13th, the New Zealanders took part in another major operation the following day: Vunakanau runway and gun positions were bombed by 24 SBDs and 24 TBFs. Half the SBDs were from the Squadron, which was leading, and several direct hits were made. Just after leaving the target two gunners saw six Japanese fighters about 5 miles away. They were doing slow rolls and steep climbing turns and made no attempt to intercept!

The two following days, the Squadron dispatched SBDs over North Bougainville and the Tobera area, before the last day of operations on 17 May. Two missions were carried out that day, the last being in the afternoon, when five aircraft (one came back early due mechanical trouble - NZ5052, Flight Sergeants L.H. Jolly and R.F. Bailey) led by the CO took off to bomb the supply area near Buka airfield. Later two New Zealand crews flew American SBDs "115" and "110" on reconnaissance missions in the East Bougainville area.

### Leaving the War Zone

On 20 May, the surviving aircraft were ferried to Renarde Field on the Russell Islands by their crews, and handed back to the Marine Corps. Most aircraft had flown about 120 hours, and to the astonishment of the receiving officer, were in "as-new" condition! This was indeed a tribute to the men of No. 25 Servicing unit who had toiled away in sometimes atrocious conditions, and with few supplies of spare parts.

After eight weeks of almost daily combat, the squadron had flown over 530 sorties totalling 1,500 flying hours in operations. It dropped 280 tons of bombs, fired 108,000 rounds of 12.7mm and 217 rounds of 7.62mm. On the debit side, the Squadron lost two aircraft as a direct result of enemy action plus three more while engaged on operations. The Squadron was disbanded at the end of May 1944. Despite its many sterling qualities, the SBD was a pre-war design and was no longer regarded as a front-line aircraft.

The next day, the crews were flown back to Whenuapai in New Zealand in two Dakotas from No. 40 Squadron RNZAF, where No.25 Squadron was disbanded on 19 June.

No.25 Squadron was re-formed at Ardmore on 30 October as a fighter squadron, and training commenced on F4U-1 Corsairs. All the remaining SBD-3's and 4's in New Zealand were used for limited crew training until February 1944, then were placed in open storage at Hobsonville Airfield. They were sold for scrap in 1948. The only complete ex-RNZAF SBD is that held at the 'Planes of Fame' Museum in the United States.

Flight Lieutenant T.R.F Johnson - Flight Sgt R.J. Howell heading for another target flying their usual aircraft, NZ5049.
(*Brendon Deere Collection*)

On 14 May 1944, 12 No. 25 Sqn SBDs were sent to strike Vunakanau runway with 12 USMC SBDs and 24 TBFs. This photograph was taken on the way to the target. The three nearest Dauntlesses are NZ5049 (F/L T.R.F. Johnson - F/Sgt R.J. Howell), NZ5068 on his left (F/O A.W.B. Hayman - Sgt D.H. Wilkie) and on his right NZ5065 (F/Sgt W.O. Nicholson - F/Sgt R.W. Cullen). In the distance are; NZ5057 (S/L T.J. ML.T. Sewell McLean de Lange - F/O L.T. Sewell), leading the formation, NZ5064 on his left (F/O B.N. Graham - F/Sgt O.E. Watson) and NZ5048 (F/O G.C. Howie - F/Sgt J.S.R. Roberston) on his right.
*(Air Force Museum PR3262)*

This has been identified as NZ5062.

The surviving pilots of No.25 Squadron were transferred to the eight RNZAF squadrons equipped with F4U Corsairs and began another operational tour. Two ex-25 Squadron pilots, flying Corsairs were killed later in the war, T.R.F. Johnson and G.C. Howie.

The war in the Pacific ended on 15 August 1945.

Flying Officer F.G. McKenzie and his gunner Pilot Officer G.H. French were among the four SBD crews (a fifth returned due to mechanical trouble) who performed the last sorties on 17 May 1944. They flew NZ5065 on that occasion, not their regular mount NZ5061, on which they are posing. (*Air Force Museum PR3439*)

## No. 25 Servicing Unit

Under the wartime system each operational Squadron had a Servicing Unit (SU) which was often, though not always, numbered the same. This unit took care of all but the major overhaul and repairs a squadron's aircraft might require. In the case of No. 25 Squadron the maintenance personnel were initially posted into the Squadron itself. Many were from the Army Co-op Squadron at Onerahi and some already had experience servicing US SBDs in the Pacific. Faced with the formidable task of keeping the well-worn SBD-3s serviceable for training flights the men set to work with few and poor facilities at first.

On 23 November No. 25 Squadron lost all its maintenance staff who were posted to the newly formed No. 25 SU under the command of Flying Officer A. Hamilton. This of course was a paper transaction and made little difference to the daily tasks of the men. With the end of training in sight, two-thirds of the SU, A & B Flights, embarked for Santo on board USS *OCTANS*, on 6 December, arriving at their new Base Depot on the 12th. Their task was to prepare the SBDs for the Squadron's arrival. C Flight moved to Santo by air in January 1944.

On completion of the aircrew operational training at Santo, the SU moved by ship to Piva and set up camp ready for the Squadron's arrival. They arrived at Piva on 9 March to find the area subjected to continual shelling by day and night. In spite of this the men worked towards the successful completion of their task and were ready for the SBD-5s when they arrived. The immediate launching into operations of the aircraft gave a large boost to the morale of the SU. Not only could they see their aircraft in action, but after weeks of shelling, when they were powerless to hit back, they could now retaliate.

Over the next eight weeks the SU members worked tirelessly to keep the aircraft serviceable. Only once did they fail to provide the number of aircraft asked for - they were one short - after a mission when one aircraft was shot down and another eight damaged. Throughout the operational tour the overall serviceability rate was 95%, an exceptionally high figure.

The CO and aircrew had (and still have) nothing but praise for the efforts of the men of No. 25 SU. Eloquent testimony was contained in the remarks of the American commander who accepted the aircraft when they were handed back after the tour. His remarks were to the effect that as far as he was concerned the Kiwis had handed back brand new aircraft! Flight time on each one was around 120 hours. The SU remained to service other RNZAF aircraft after the departure of the Squadron, as SU's remained in the forward area for longer periods than the Squadrons. They were relieved by personnel rotation rather than the block movement common to aircrew.

No. 25 SU personnel preparing SBD-4 NZ5034 for another training flight at Espiritu Santo (New Hebrides) in February 1944.
(*Peter Mossong Collection*)

## SOME OF NO. 25 SQUADRON CREWS IN 1944

Above :
Flying Officer L.H.F. Brown and Flight Sergeant G.D. Ashworth - SBD-5 NZ5047. (*Air Force Museum PR3449*)
Below :
Sergeant P.R.B. Symonds and Flight Sergeant B. Boden - SBD-5 NZ5059. (*Air Force Museum PR3444*)

Above :
Flight Sergeant C.M. O'Neil and Flight Sergeant D.W. Gray - SBD-5 NZ5056 (*Air Force Museum PR3441*)
Below :
Flight Sergeant L.H. Jolly and Flight Sergeant T.E Price - SBD-5 NZ5054. (*Air Force Museum PR3440*)

Above :
Flight Sergeant N.L. Kelly and Flight Sergeant B.E. Cullen - SBD-5 NZ5062 (*Air Force Museum PR3442*)
Below :
Sergeant C.G.W. Kuhn and Flight Sergeant M. Small - SBD-5 NZ5053. (*Air Force Museum PR3446*)

# The Operational Record

Dauntlesses of No. 25 Squadron and the USMC ready to take-off for another mission. In the foreground is NZ5062 flown by Flight Sergeants N.L. Kelly and B.E. Cullen. Just ahead is another SBD from the Squadron with an extra-large fuselage

## Operational Diary - Number of Sorties

| Month | Sorties | Hours flown [1] |
|---|---|---|
| 24.03.44 | 19 | 22.6 |
| 25.03.44 | 23 | 20.8 |
| 26.03.44 | 12 | 12.0 |
| 27.03.44 | 12 | 30.4 |
| 28.03.44 | 11 | 35.6 |
| 29.03.44 | 6 | 21.9 |
| 30.03.44 | 12 | 46.9 |
| 01.04.44 | 12 | 13.2 |
| 02.04.44 | 12 | 44.3 |
| 03.04.44 | 12 | 40.1 |
| 06.04.44 | 11 | 40.3 |
| 07.04.44 | 6 | 22.9 |
| 08.04.44 | 11 | 28.9 |
| 09.04.44 | 12 | 42.4 |
| 10.04.44 | 12 | 38.1 |
| 11.04.44 | 12 | 43.2 |
| 12.04.44 | 12 | 44.2 |
| 13.04.44 | 18 | 61.1 |
| 15.04.44 | 12 | 43.7 |
| 16.04.44 | 12 | 44.2 |
| 17.04.44 | 12 | 40.2 |
| 18.04.44 | 5 | 19.7 |
| 19.04.44 | 9 | 29.7 |
| 21.04.44 | 12 | 24.0 |
| 22.04.44 | 12 | 44.2 |
| 23.04.44 | 12 | 5.3 |
| 25.04.44 | 12 | 40.8 |
| 26.04.44 | 12 | 33.0 |
| 28.04.44 | 12 | 39.6 |
| 29.04.44 | 12 | 30.9 |
| 01.05.44 | 12 | 20.5 |
| 02.05.44 | 12 | 43.6 |
| 03.05.44 | 12 | 43.3 |
| 04.05.44 | 12 | 20.6 |
| 05.05.44 | 12 | 23.1 |
| 06.05.44 | 12 | 42.2 |
| 07.05.44 | 16 | 35.7 |
| 08.05.44 | 6 | 11.0 |
| 10.05.44 | 12 | 33.9 |
| 11.05.44 | 12 | 38.9 |
| 12.05.44 | 12 | 25.2 |
| 13.05.44 | 2 | 3.8 |
| 14.05.44 | 12 | 41.2 |
| 15.05.44 | 13 | 21.0 |
| 16.05.44 | 9 | 21.1 |
| 17.05.44 | 11 | 27.5 |

Total:
536 sorties
1,457.4 hours

### First and last sortie planned

| date | Mission | Time in/out |
|---|---|---|
| 24.03.44 | Artillery Spotting | 1155-1430 |

Aircraft and Crew :
NZ5051 (F/L J.W. Edwards - Sgt Barter USMC)
NZ5059 (F/Sgt P.Symonds - Lt Schnepel USMC)

| 17.05.44 | Strike Burka Airfield | 1420-1630 |

Aircraft and Crew :
NZ5057 (S/L T.J.De Lange - F/O L.T.Sewell)
NZ5048 (F/O G.C. Howie - F/Sgt J.Roberston)
NZ5064 (F/O B.N.Graham - F/Sgt O.E.Watson)
NZ5065 (F/O F.G.McKenzie - P/O G.H.French)
NZ5052 (F/Sgt L.H.Jolly - F/Sgt R.F.Bailey)

[1] Time for aircraft which failed to return is not included.

### Known number of sortie completed by each SBD-5

| Serial | First sortie | Last sortie | Nb Sortie | Not completed | Op.hours | Comment |
|---|---|---|---|---|---|---|
| NZ5046 | 24.03.44 | 16.05.44 | 30 | 3 | 85.2 | |
| NZ5047 | 24.03.44 | 15.05.44 | 34 | 2 | 90.6 | |
| NZ5048 | 24.03.44 | 17.05.44 | 40 | 3 | 107.1 | |
| NZ5049 | 24.03.44 | 17.05.44 | 23 | 3 | 70.7 | |
| NZ5050 | 24.03.44 | 17.04.44 | 15 | 1 | 47.1 | Lost on its 16th sortie |
| NZ5051 | 24.03.44 | 10.05.44 | 27 | 1 | 77.1 | Lost on its 28th sortie |
| NZ5052 | 24.03.44 | 17.05.44 | 29 | 4 | 88.2 | |
| NZ5053 | 25.03.44 | 17.05.44 | 10 | 3 | 31.0 | |
| NZ5054 | 25.03.44 | 02.04.44 | 6 | 1 | 12.5 | Crashed on return |
| NZ5055 | - | - | - | - | - | Crashed on ferry flight |
| NZ5056 | 27.03.44 | 16.05.44 | 31 | 2 | 89.3 | |
| NZ5057 | 24.03.44 | 17.05.44 | 36 | 1 | 101.6 | |
| NZ5058 | 24.03.44 | 17.04.44 | 11 | 2 | 38.5 | |
| NZ5059 | 24.03.44 | 02.04.44 | 7 | 1 | 17.8 | Crashed on return |
| NZ5060 | 24.03.44 | 11.05.44 | 32 | 2 | 95.9 | |
| NZ5061 | 24.03.44 | 16.05.44 | 33 | 3 | 94.7 | |
| NZ5062 | 24.03.44 | 17.05.44 | 28 | 3 | 89.3 | |
| NZ5063 | 08.04.44 | 17.05.44 | 23 | 1 | 62.2 | |
| NZ5064 | 01.04.44 | 17.05.44 | 25 | 1 | 76.0 | |
| NZ5065 | 03.04.44 | 17.05.44 | 25 | 1 | 67.3 | |
| NZ5066 | 13.04.44 | 16.05.44 | 24 | 3 | 68.9 | |
| NZ5067 | 26.04.44 | 16.05.44 | 12 | - | 32.0 | |
| NZ5068 | 28.04.44 | 14.05.44 | 11 | - | 26.9 | |

**Notes :**
Also, two other sorties were performed with a mixed crew NZ/US on USMC aircraft 177 and 181 on 25 March 1944.

Last check before take-off for NZ5056, the regular mount of Flight Sergeants C.N. O'Neill and D.W. Gray.

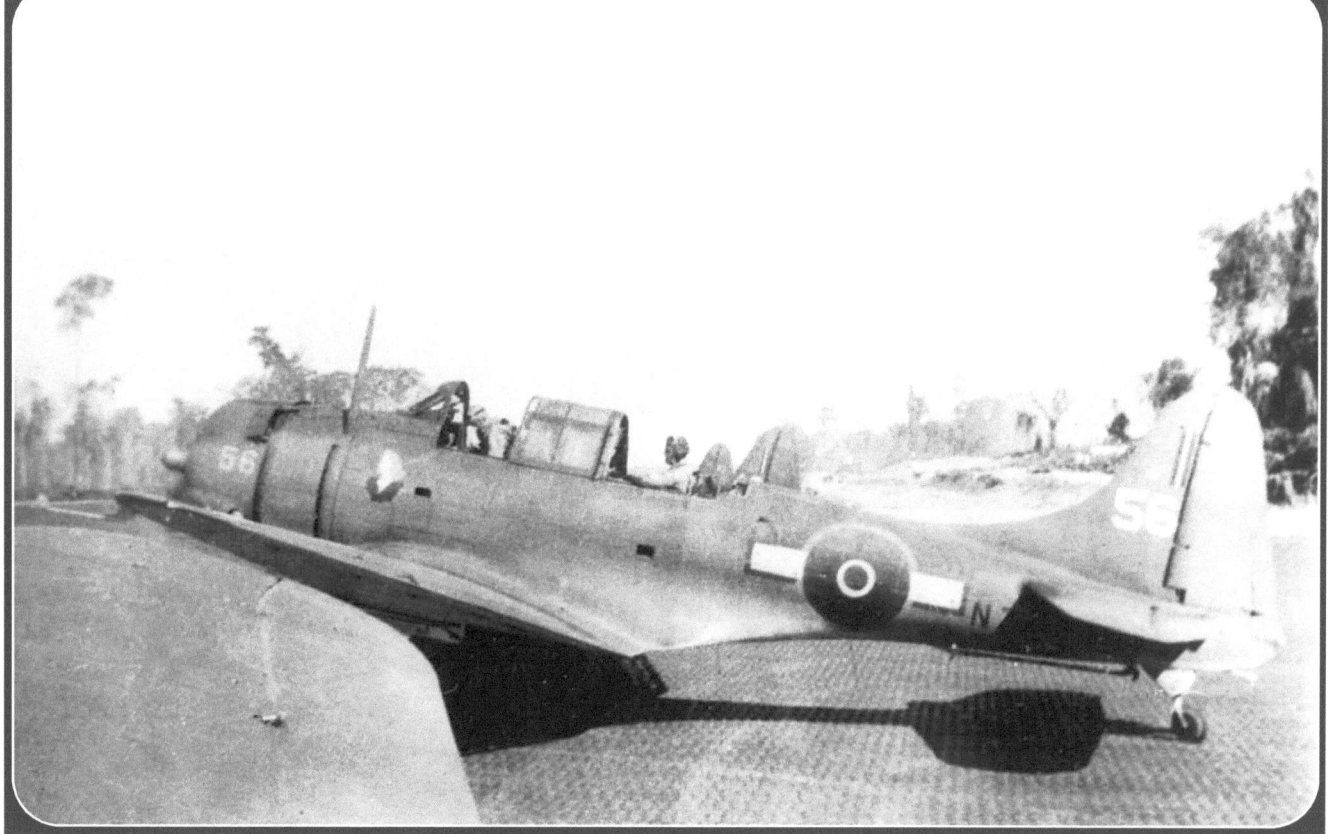

## Aircraft Lost on Operations
### No. 25 Squadron, RNZAF

| Date | Crew | SN | Origin | Serial | Fate | Cause |
|---|---|---|---|---|---|---|
| 02.04.44 | F/Sgt Leslie H. **Jolly** | NZ42410 | RNZAF | NZ5054 | - | 3 |
| | F/Sgt Thomas E. **Price** | NZ411045 | RNZAF | | - | |
| | Sgt Peter R.B. **Symonds** | NZ424218 | RNZAF | NZ5059 | - | 3 |
| | F/Sgt Belie **Boden** | NZ41303 | RNZAF | | - | |
| 17.04.44 | P/O Geoffrey H. **Cray** | NZ4213648 | RNZAF | NZ5050 | † | 2 |
| | F/Sgt Frank D. **Bell** | NZ413244 | RNZAF | | † | |
| | Sgt Alfred C.L. **Forsberg** | NZ4212702 | RNZAF | NZ5058 | - | 2 |
| | F/Sgt Edward G. **Leatham** | NZ413263 | RNZAF | | - | |
| 10.05.44 | F/L Jack W. **Edwards** | NZ39908 | RNZAF | NZ5051 | † | 2 |
| | W/O Louis A. **Hoppe** | NZ415533 | RNZAF | | † | |

Causes : *1 Enemy aircraft, 2 Flak, 3 Unknown or other causes.*

## Total : 5

Flight Lieutenant J.W. Edwards (right) and Warrant Officer L.A. Hoppe in front of their regular mount, NZ5051. Note the individual marking and the simplified squadron badge. (*Air Force Museum PR3466*)

## Aircraft Lost by Accident
### No. 25 Squadron, RNZAF

| Date | Crew | SN | Origin | Serial | Fate |
|---|---|---|---|---|---|
| 13.09.43 | P/O William D. McJannet | NZ421249 | RNZAF | NZ211 | † |
|  | Sgt Douglas M.J. Cairns | NZ422687 | RNZAF |  | † |
| 19.01.44 | P/O R.S. McIntosh | NZ4213676 | RNZAF | NZ5004 [1] | - |
| 11.02.44 | P/O Alexander Moore | NZ416523 | RNZAF | NZ5037 | † |
|  | F/Sgt John K. Munro | NZ417229 | RNZAF |  | † |
| 22.03.44 | P/O B.N. Graham | NZ416109 | RNZAF | NZ5055 | - |
|  | Sgt Olver E. Watson | NZ414365 | RNZAF |  | - |
| 04.04.44 | F/O Leslie A. McLellan-Symonds | NZ401314 | RNZAF | BuNo. 28452 | PoW |

*Total: 5*

[1] At this time NZ5004 was listed as being with No. 26 Squadron, a unit that was never quite formed. Damage to the aircraft was initially listed as category "C", but later changed to category "E", a write off.

An uncomfortable position for SBD-4 NZ5024, after it swung on landing, 15 December 1943 at Seagrove. Except for one fatal accident which cost two lives, training in New Zealand was relatively trouble free. A handful of minor accidents were recorded; NZ5017 on 28.11.43 - damaged by gunfire, NZ5013 on 29.11.43 - engine failure, NZ5026 on 11.12.43 - damaged during gun test and NZ5004 - damaged on landing. At Espiritu Santo, one more minor accident was recorded on 18.02.44 when NZ5029's brakes failed on landing. (*Brendon Deere Collection*)

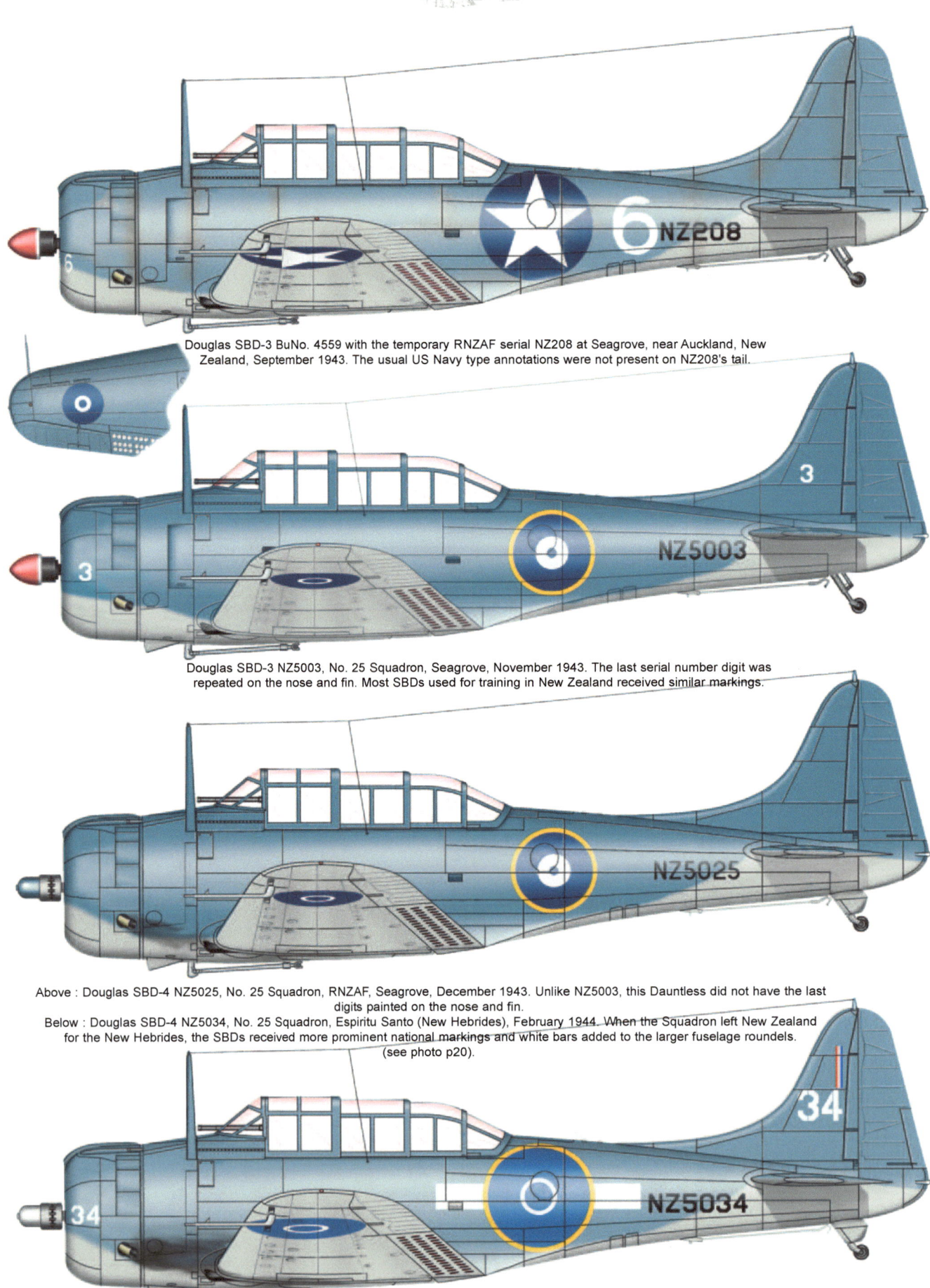

Douglas SBD-3 BuNo. 4559 with the temporary RNZAF serial NZ208 at Seagrove, near Auckland, New Zealand, September 1943. The usual US Navy type annotations were not present on NZ208's tail.

Douglas SBD-3 NZ5003, No. 25 Squadron, Seagrove, November 1943. The last serial number digit was repeated on the nose and fin. Most SBDs used for training in New Zealand received similar markings.

Above : Douglas SBD-4 NZ5025, No. 25 Squadron, RNZAF, Seagrove, December 1943. Unlike NZ5003, this Dauntless did not have the last digits painted on the nose and fin.
Below : Douglas SBD-4 NZ5034, No. 25 Squadron, Espiritu Santo (New Hebrides), February 1944. When the Squadron left New Zealand for the New Hebrides, the SBDs received more prominent national markings and white bars added to the larger fuselage roundels.
(see photo p20).

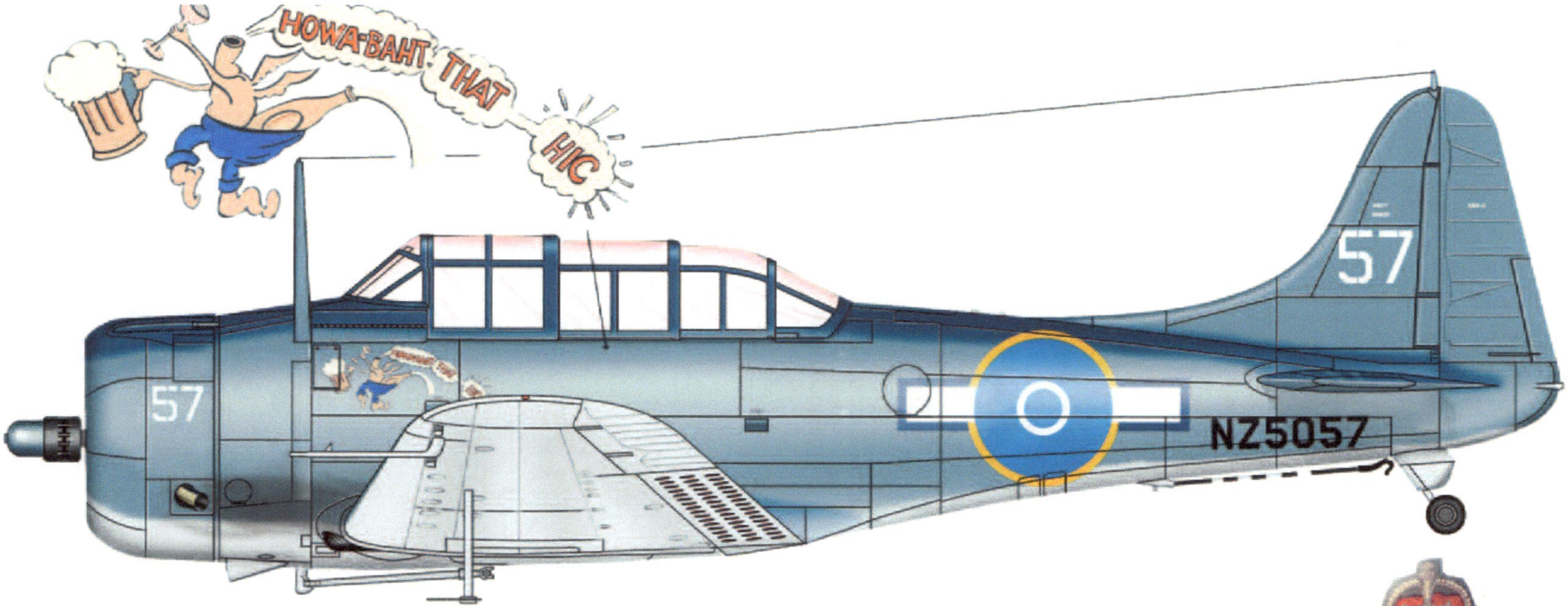

Douglas SBD-5 NZ5057, No. 25 Squadron, RNZAF, Squadron Leader T.J. McLean de Lange / Flying Officer L.T. Sewell, Henderson Field, Guadalcanal, Solomon Islands, March 1944.

Note that for all SBD-5 allocated to the Squadron, the USN annotations were remained painted on the tail ("NAVY" and the BuNo on the fin, "SBD-5" on the rudder). This aircraft is the only one known to have a full colour Squadron badge painted on the right side. The colour photograph on the right of a panel saved from NZ5057 has deteriorated.

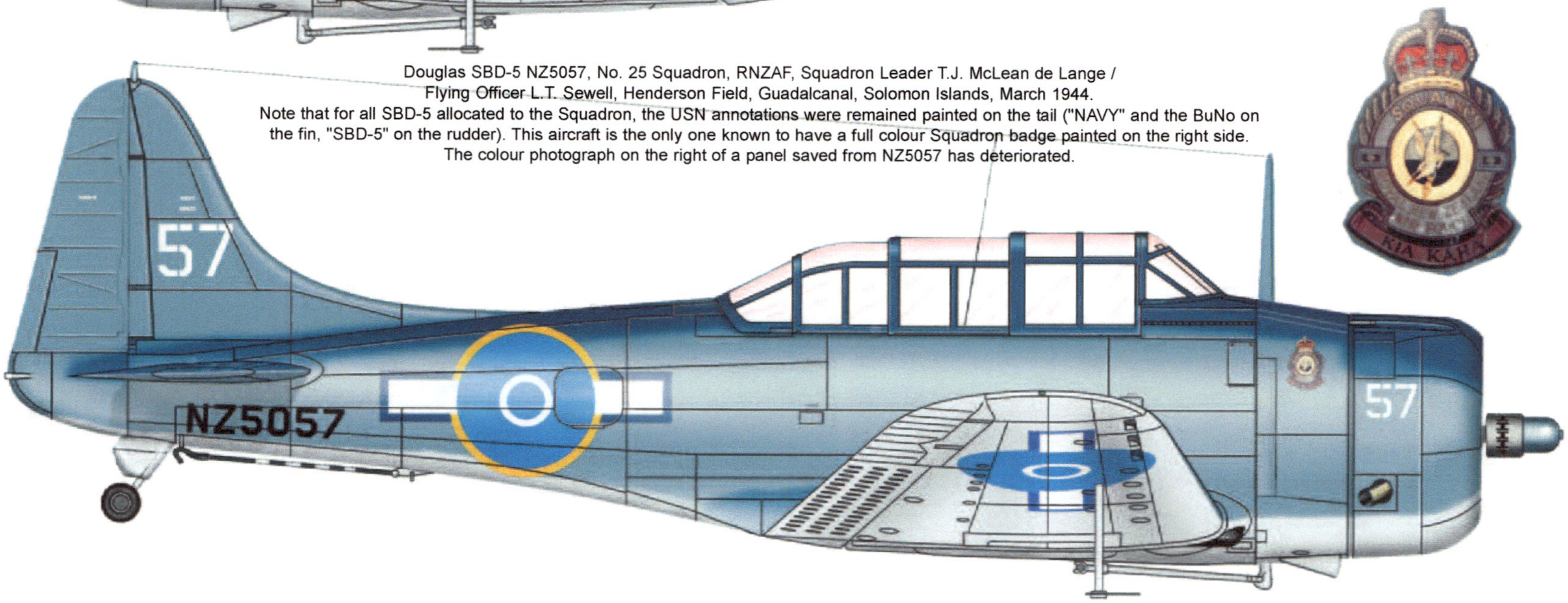

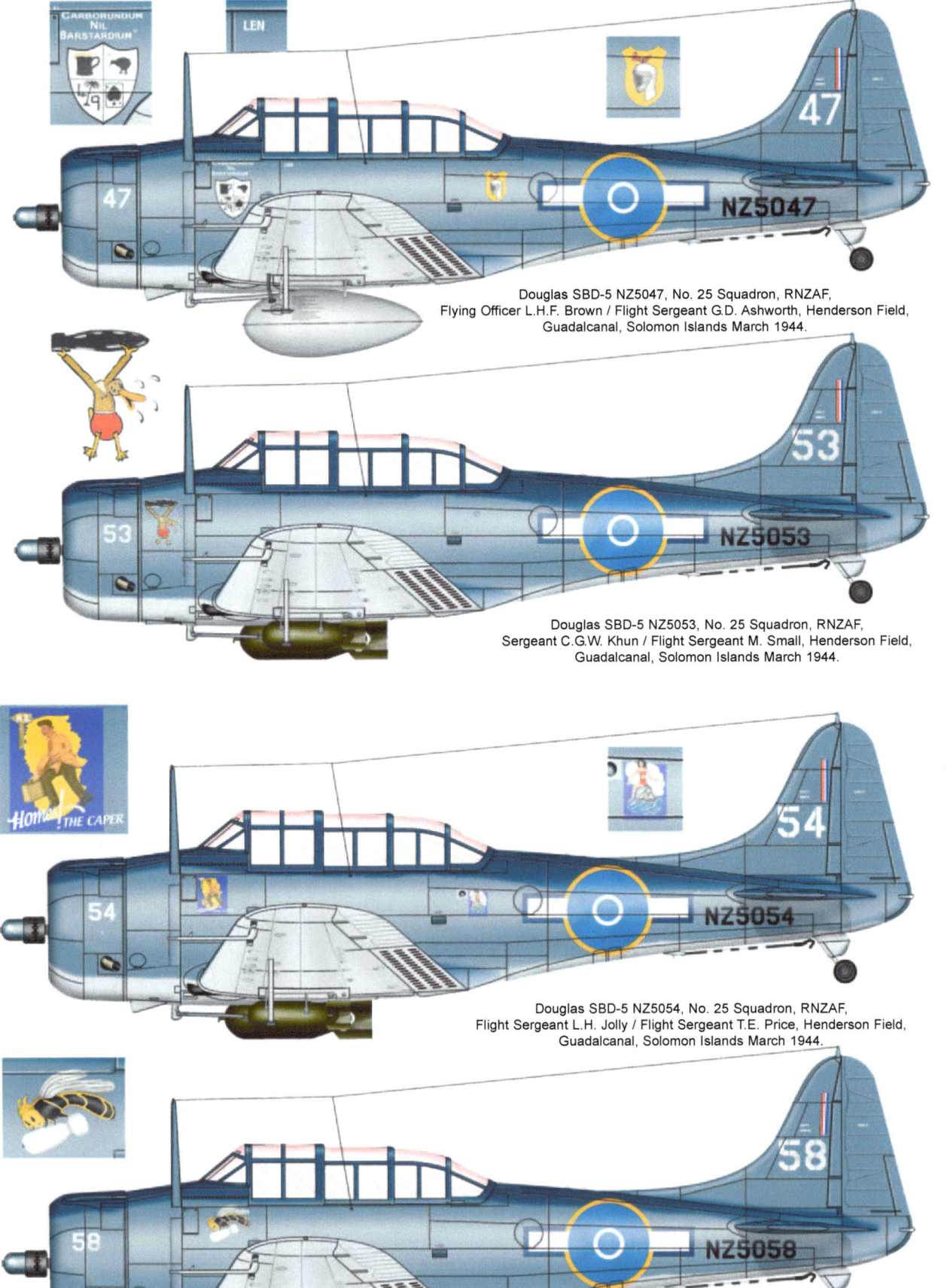

Douglas SBD-5 NZ5047, No. 25 Squadron, RNZAF,
Flying Officer L.H.F. Brown / Flight Sergeant G.D. Ashworth, Henderson Field,
Guadalcanal, Solomon Islands March 1944.

Douglas SBD-5 NZ5053, No. 25 Squadron, RNZAF,
Sergeant C.G.W. Khun / Flight Sergeant M. Small, Henderson Field,
Guadalcanal, Solomon Islands March 1944.

Douglas SBD-5 NZ5054, No. 25 Squadron, RNZAF,
Flight Sergeant L.H. Jolly / Flight Sergeant T.E. Price, Henderson Field,
Guadalcanal, Solomon Islands March 1944.

Douglas SBD-5 NZ5058, No. 25 Squadron, RNZAF,
Sergeant A.C.L. Forsberg / Flight Sergeant E.G. Leatham, Henderson Field,
Guadalcanal, Solomon Islands March 1944.

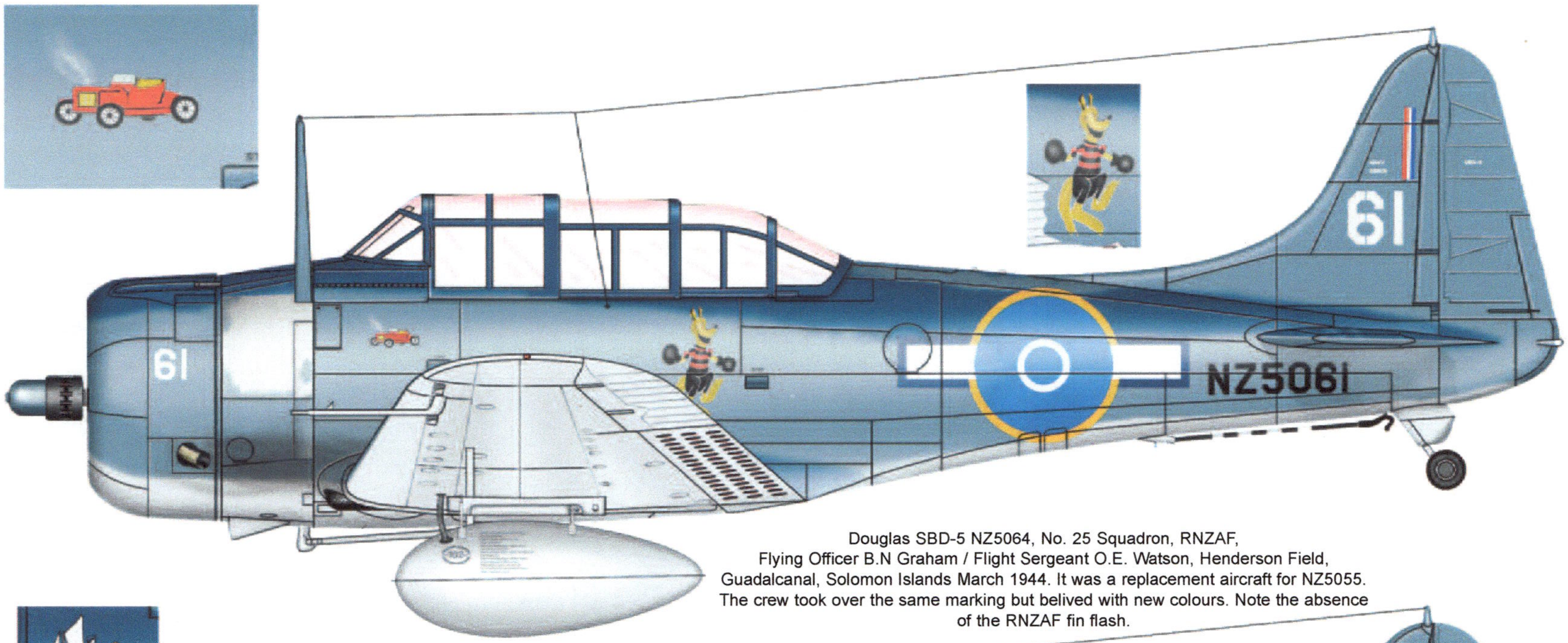

Douglas SBD-5 NZ5064, No. 25 Squadron, RNZAF, Flying Officer B.N Graham / Flight Sergeant O.E. Watson, Henderson Field, Guadalcanal, Solomon Islands March 1944. It was a replacement aircraft for NZ5055. The crew took over the same marking but belived with new colours. Note the absence of the RNZAF fin flash.

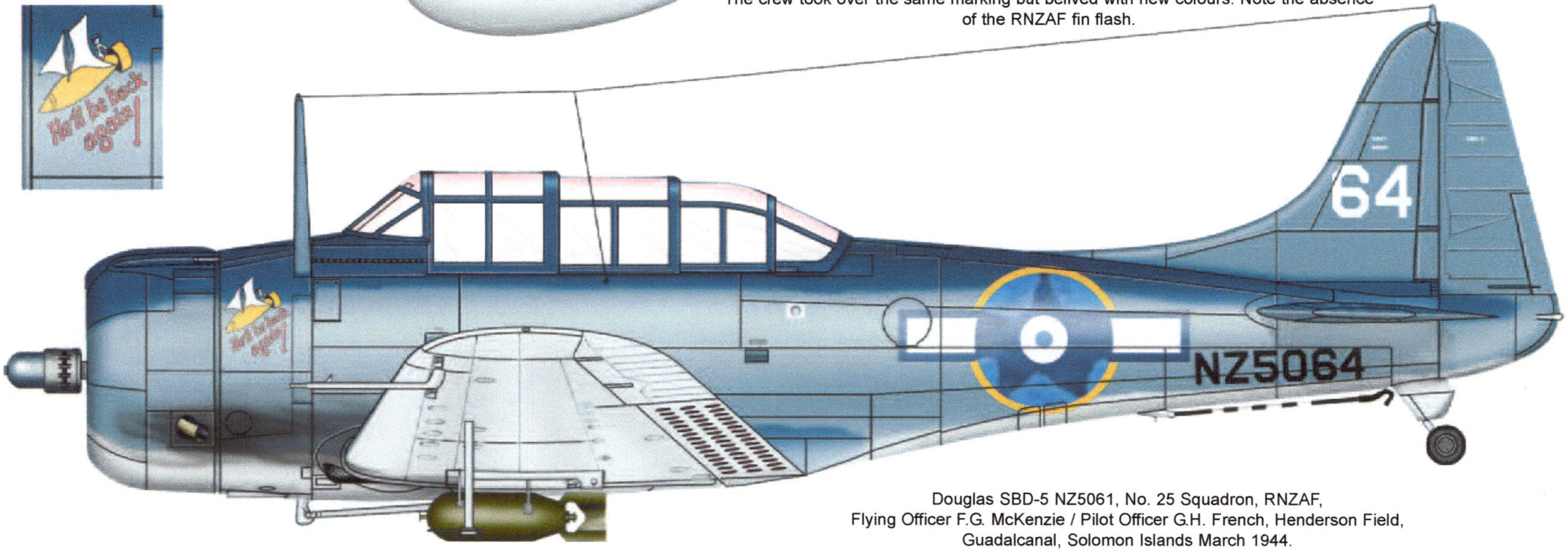

Douglas SBD-5 NZ5061, No. 25 Squadron, RNZAF, Flying Officer F.G. McKenzie / Pilot Officer G.H. French, Henderson Field, Guadalcanal, Solomon Islands March 1944.

## SOME MORE INDIVIDUAL MARKINGS

Left : Individual marking for NZ5049 of Flight Lieutenant T.R.F. Johnson / Flight Sergeant R.J. Howell.
Right : Individual marking for NZ5055, as flown by Flying Officer B.N. Graham / Flight Sergeant O.E. Watson, who later flew NZ5064 and applied a very similar personal marking.
Below : Top view and scrap bottom view applicable to all No. 25 Squadron's SBD-5s.

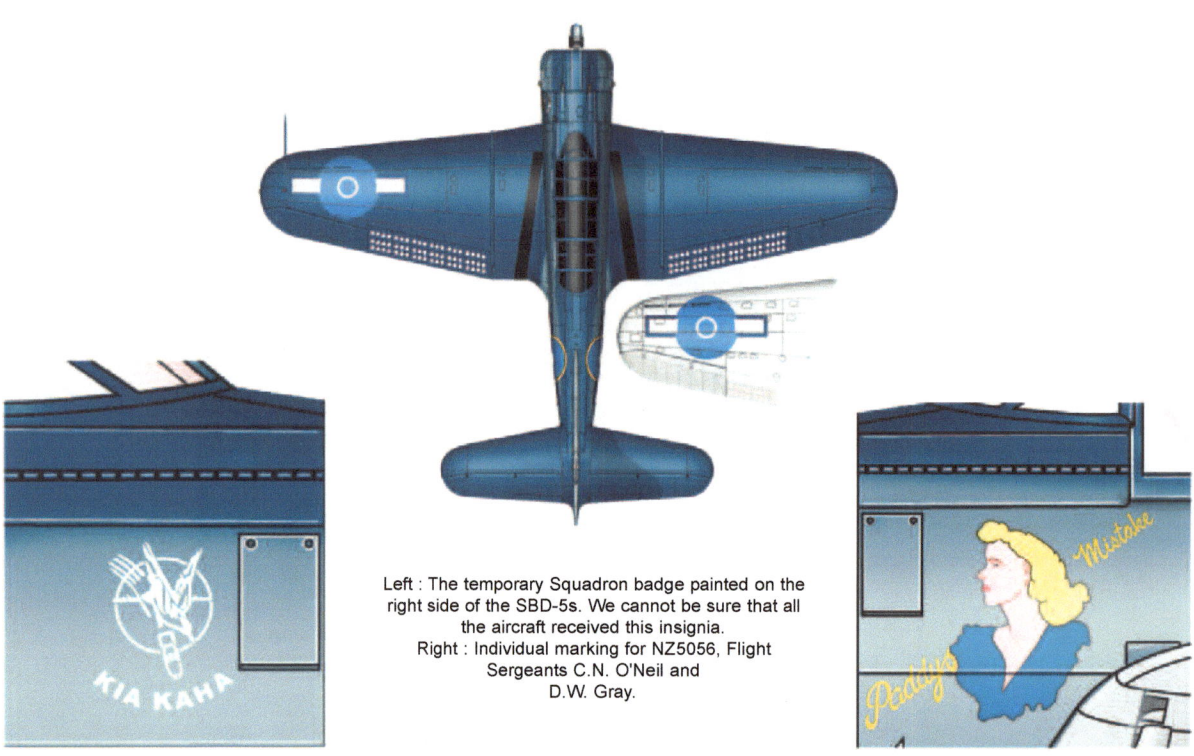

Left : The temporary Squadron badge painted on the right side of the SBD-5s. We cannot be sure that all the aircraft received this insignia.
Right : Individual marking for NZ5056, Flight Sergeants C.N. O'Neil and D.W. Gray.

Right : Individual marking of NZ5059, Sergeant P.R.B. Symonds / Flight Sergeant B. Boden.

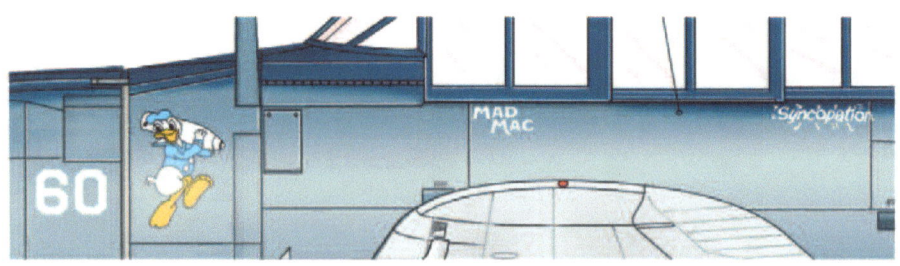

Left : Individual marking of NZ5060, Flying Officer L.A. McLellan-Symonds / Flight Sergeant R.F. Bailey, with the inscriptions, "MAD MAC" and "SYNCOPATION" painted below the cockpit.

†

## Roll of Honour

| Name | Rank | Age | Origin | Date | Serial |
|---|---|---|---|---|---|
| **BELL**, Frank Desmond | F/Sgt | 22 | RNZAF | 17.04.44 | NZ5050 |
| **CAIRNS**, Douglas Martin James | Sgt | 20 | RNZAF | 13.09.43 | NZ211 |
| **CRAY,** Geoffrey Haughton | P/O | 21 | RNZAF | 17.04.44 | NZ5050 |
| **EDWARDS**, Jack Ward | F/L | 28 | RNZAF | 10.05.44 | NZ5051 |
| **HOPPE**, Louis Andreas | W/O | 25 | RNZAF | 10.05.44 | NZ5051 |
| **McJANNET**, William David | P/O | 32 | RNZAF | 13.09.43 | NZ211 |
| **McLELLAN-SYMONDS**, Leslie Alexander [1] | F/O | 33 | RNZAF | 25.05.44 | - |
| **MOORE**, Alexander | P/O | 24 | RNZAF | 11.02.44 | NZ5037 |
| **MUNRO**, John Keith | F/Sgt | 22 | RNZAF | 11.02.44 | NZ5037 |

[1] Died in captivity.

***Total: 9***

NZ5064 was a replacement aircraft for NZ5055 which crashed at Henderson Field on 22 March 1944. The same individual markings were applied on NZ5064. Note the US white star still visible under the RNZAF roundel. (*Brendon Deere Collection*)

## With the British

The Royal Navy acquired a small number of SBD-5, essentially to carry out trials of the DBS-1 bombsight which was also fitted to the Dauntless' successor, the Curtiss SB2C Helldiver, which was expected to enter Fleet Air Arm service. The first arrived in the UK in November 1943. In all, nine flew under British markings.

| | | |
|---|---|---|
| **JS997** | ex-BuNo 36022 | Accepted USN Sep-43 and served between November 1943 and August 1945 at least. |
| **JS998** | ex-BuNo 36023 | Accepted USN Sep-43. Stored at 51 MU as spare aircraft but eventually was used at SF Eastleigh between March 1945 and July 1946. |
| **JS999** | ex-BuNo 36456 | Accepted USN Nov-43. Stored at 51 MU at first then used for various test flights at Farnborough between March and July 1944. Then issued to No. 787 Sqn. Suffered an accident on 31.07.44 following an undercarriage failure. Not repaired. |
| **JT923** | ex-BuNo 54191 | Accepted USN Jan-44. Initially stored then issued to SF Eastleigh by August 1945. Suffered an engine failure on take-off on 20.06.46 and crashed. The aircraft was declared not repairable. |
| **JT924** | ex-BuNo 54192 | Accepted USN Jan-44. Stored at No. 51 MU then went to the RAF in April 1945. Used until Feb-46 then stored at No. 34 MU. SOC 15.10.46. |
| **JT925** | ex-BuNo 54193 | Accepted USN Jan-44. Stored at No. 5 MU, then went to the RAF in April 1945. Used until Feb-46 then stored at No. 34 MU. SOC 15.10.46. |
| **JT926** | ex-BuNo 54194 | Accepted USN Jan-44. Stored at No. 51 MU, then to RAF on 08.06.44 at Handling Squadron. Later stored at No. 15 MU. SOC 30.03.45. |
| **JT927** | ex-BuNo 54195 | Accepted USN Jan-44. Stored at No. 51 MU then to No. 700 Sqn between December 44 and February 1946. |
| **JT928** | ex-BuNo 54196 | Accepted USN Jan-44. Stored at No. 51 MU, then used at the RAE between 13.08.44 and 02.10.44 when it was issued to No. 787 Sqn, but returned to the RAE on 10.10.44, then back to 787 Sqn on 14.10.44. Again with RAE between 09.12.44 and 29.03.46, then stored and probably SOC soon afterwards. |

A further allocation of fourteen more aircraft was cancelled, and the serial numbers JT929-JT962 which had been reserved for further aircraft, to a total of 43, were not used.

Douglas SBD-8 JS997 seen at Boscombe Down in December 1943 for trails of its dive-bombing sight.

www.ingramcontent.com/pod-product-compliance
Lightning Source LLC
LaVergne TN
LVHW070347090426
835510LV00036B/66